T0195944

I HAVE A HEARING LOSS, AND IT'S OKAY!

Written by
Dr. William M. Bauer

Illustrated by
Mallory Hill

WestBow Press books may be ordered through booksellers or by contacting:

WestBow Press
A Division of Thomas Nelson & Zondervan
1663 Liberty Drive
Bloomington, IN 47403
www.westbowpress.com
844-714-3454

Interior Image Credit: Mallory Hill

ISBN: 978-1-6642-4512-9 (sc)
ISBN: 978-1-6642-4511-2 (e)

Library of Congress Control Number: 2021919120

Print information available on the last page.

WestBow Press rev. date: 09/24/2021

WESTBOW
P R E S S®
A DIVISION OF THOMAS NELSON
& ZONDERVAN

I HAVE A HEARING LOSS, AND
IT'S OKAY!

About the Author:

Dr. William M. (Bill) Bauer is a licensed clinical counselor in the rural Mid-Ohio Valley area who was a former classroom teacher, principal, and college professor. He has worked with children and adults with disabilities all of his life and hopes that this book brings an understanding to children with disabilities, their teachers, and their classmates. Dr. Bauer was born with a severe hearing impairment.

THIS BOOK IS DEDICATED TO:

ALL PEOPLE WITH DISABILITIES WHOSE LIVES ARE SHARED IN THIS BOOK SERIES TO MAKE THE WORLD A BETTER PLACE. ALL WE WANT IS TO BE ACCEPTED AS WE ARE, HAVE FRIENDS, LIVE IN OUR COMMUNITIES AND TO DREAM AS OUR NON-DISABLED PEERS.

SPECIAL THANKS TO MY WIFE, MARY ELLA, DAUGHTER MADISON RYSER, HER HUSBAND ANDREW AND GRANDSON JACK.

#GRANTSPEED.
LOVE YOU, SON

Forewords:

I have had the pleasure of working with Dr. Bauer in the professional education and mental health fields for over two decades, and this book series is his latest outstanding work to help young people understand and accept differences. Each title focuses on a uniqueness and assures us that "it is OKAY!"

Dr. Stephanie Starcher
Public School Superintendent

Being different is OK! Every effort to erase stigma surrounding our differences is important. The earlier we start, the better chance we have at preventing stigma from even occurring. I had the honor of meeting Dr. Bill Bauer when I was in college, and it is no surprise his work as a mental health advocate would transpire into this series of books. I'm thankful for his commitment to celebrating our differences.

Nick Gehlfuss, MFA, Actor, film and television.
Currently, Dr. Halstead, Chicago Med.

This book series by Dr. William Bauer — my good friend Bill — fills a niche in children's literature that embraces diversity and self-esteem. This series is not only important, but extremely fun. As founder of Orphans International, I look forward to reading these stories to children of all faiths and abilities around the world. This book is indeed a living testament to Bill's own son. The world is a better place because of Bill Bauer! #GrantSpeed

James Jay Dudley Luce, Founder Orphans International Worldwide,
International Entrepreneur

HI!
MY NAME IS BILLY, AND I HAVE A HEARING LOSS.

DID YOU KNOW THERE ARE TWO TYPES OF HEARING LOSS? PEOPLE WHO CAN'T HEAR AT ALL (DEAF) AND THOSE THAT CAN HEAR SOME (HARD-OF-HEARING).

EMMA   BILLY   JERRI

I CAN'T HEAR AS WELL AS MY FRIENDS, SO I HAVE TO WEAR A HEARING AID TO HEAR.

SOME PEOPLE WHO ARE HARD OF HEARING OR DEAF CAN READ LIPS, AND SOME DO SIGN LANGUAGE. I AM REALLY GOOD AT READING LIPS.

MOST PEOPLE WHO ARE DEAF USE THEIR HANDS TO TALK TO OTHERS. THIS IS CALLED SIGN LANGUAGE. I USE MY OWN VOICE TO TALK.

I USUALLY SIT IN THE FRONT OF THE CLASSROOM SO I CAN SEE THE TEACHER AND TELL HER WHAT I NEED. I AM USUALLY OKAY, BUT SOMETIMES I DON'T UNDERSTAND EVERYTHING SO I ASK THE TEACHER.

SOME PEOPLE WHO ARE HARD OF HEARING OR DEAF MAY HAVE A COCHLEAR IMPLANT TO HELP THEM HEAR.

I HAVE SPEECH THERAPY AT SCHOOL SO I CAN LEARN HOW TO TALK PROPERLY. SINCE I CAN'T HEAR SOUNDS LIKE EVERYONE ELSE, I HAVE TO LEARN TO WATCH LIPS AND TALK.

WHEN I PLAY SPORTS, MY MOM AND I TELL THE COACH WHAT I CAN AND CAN'T HEAR. TEAM SPORTS ARE HARD FOR ME SO I ENJOY BEING ON A SWIM TEAM.

MY FRIENDS AT SCHOOL ARE NICE TO ME AND HELP ME. THEY UNDERSTAND ME AND WILL NOT BULLY ME IF I TALK DIFFERENTLY OR DON'T HEAR SOMETHING, BUT SOMETIMES I LAUGH AT MYSELF. IT'S ALL GOOD.

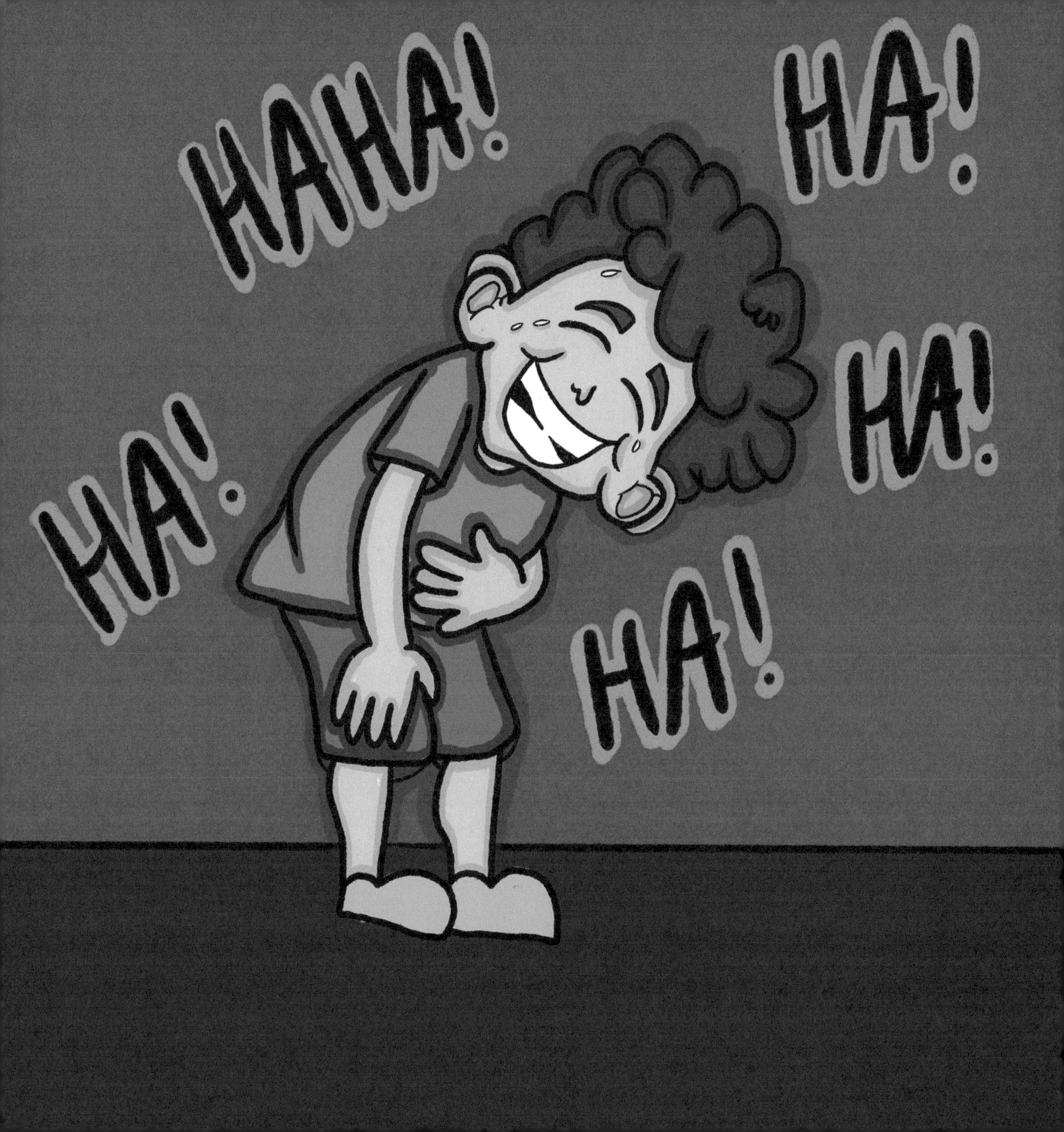
HAHA!
HA!
HA!
HA!
HA!

I HAVE A LOT OF PEOPLE IN MY LIFE WHO BELIEVE IN ME, AND I CAN BE WHAT I WANT TO BE WHEN I GROW UP.

MY NAME IS BILLY. I HAVE A HEARING LOSS, AND IT'S OKAY!

Printed in the United States
by Baker & Taylor Publisher Services